D1554908

WHEN
THE ONLY LIGHT
IS
FIRE

SAEED JONES

Alexander, Arkansas
www.siblingrivalrypress.com

Sibling Rivalry Press, LLC
13913 Magnolia Glen Drive
Alexander, AR 72002

www.siblingrivalrypress.com

ISBN: 978-1-937420-03-1

First Sibling Rivalry Press Edition, November 2011.

Acknowledgements

With gratitude to the editors of the journals in which these poems first appeared:

Ganymede – "Kudzu" & "The Fabulist" (published as "Kerry, or The Fabulist")

Emerson Review – "Terrible Boy" (published as "Terrible Child")

Hayden's Ferry Review – "Cruel Body"

Jubilat – "Blue Prelude"

Linebreak – "Isaac, After Mount Moriah"

The Collagist – "Mississippi Drowning"

Ocho – "Daedalus, After Icarus"

West Branch – "Boy at Threshold" & "After the First Shot"

Union Station Magazine – "Room 31"

Weave Magazine – "Nocturne"

Esque Magazine – "Jasper, 1998"

Contents

What's left of burning
burns as well
me down to blackened glass
an offering in anthracite

- Reginald Shepherd

Kudzu

I won't be forgiven
for what I've made
of myself.
Soil recoils
from my hooked kisses.
Pines turn their backs
on me. They know
what I can do
with the wrap of my legs.
Each summer,
when the air becomes crowded
with want, I set all my tongues
upon you.
To quiet this body,
you must answer
my tendrilled craving.
All I've ever wanted
was to kiss crevices, pry them open,
and flourish within dew-slick
hollows.
How you mistake
my affection.
And if I ever strangled sparrows,
it was only because I dreamed
of better songs.

Terrible Boy

> "...my whole life, my whole huge seven year old life."
> - Pushkin

In the field, one paw of the lion-clawed bathtub
glints in the light. Lukewarm buckets of water
carried for miles. And I will pay brightly

for this slick body. Unclean under
a back-turned sun, I sing the sins
that brought me here:

> I turned the family portrait face down
> when he was on me,

> fed gasoline to the roots of forsythia,

> broke a mirror to slim
> my reflection's waist,

> what he calls me is not my name

and I love it. Damask chair
beside the tub and on it, hand-made armor
of bone.

Out of the water, in a wet wheat towel –

I wake
in my unlit room.

Father standing at the door.

Boy in Stolen Evening Gown

In this field of thistle, I am the improbable
lady. How I wear the word: sequined weight snagging

my saunter into overgrown grass, blonde
split-end blades. I waltz in an acre of bad wigs.

Sir who is no one, sir who is yet to come, I need you
to undo this zipped back, trace the chiffon

body I've borrowed. See how I switch my hips
for you, dry grass cracking under my pretend

high heels? Call me and I'm at your side,
one wildflower behind my ear. Ask me

and I'll slip out of this softness, the dress
a black cloud at my feet.

I could be the boy wearing nothing,
a negligee of gnats.

Boy at Edge of Woods

After his gasp and *god damn*
grunt, after his zipper closes
its teeth, his tongue leaves
its shadows, leaves me
alone to pick pine needles
from my hair, to brush
leaves off my shirt as blades
of light hang from the trees,
as I re-learn my legs – mud
stained knees and walk back
to my burning house.

Isaac, After Mount Moriah

Asleep on the roof when rain comes,
water collects in the dips of his collarbone.

Dirty haired boy, my rascal, my sacrifice. Never
an easy dream. I watch him wrestle my shadow, shut eyelids
trembling, one fist ready for me.

Leave him a blanket, leave him alone.

Night before, found him caked in dirt,
sleeping in a ditch, wet black stones for pillows.

What kind of father does he make me, this boy
I find tangled in the hair of willows, curled fetal
in the grove?

Once, I found him in a far field, the mountain's peak
like a blade above us both.

Nocturne

I.

She wakes shouting *Albert,*
Albert in darkness.
The name of her father,
the name of his son.
One is dead, the other away
and neither is me: her son, the one
holding her sweat-slick hand
as she slips back into absence.

II.

I drive half-way across the bridge,
kill my engine and wait.
You told me ghosts will push
my car to the other end.
In stillness, the bridge, rusted
with the memory of use,
complains of chronic aches:
the weight of the living,
who expect the dead
to finish what we will not do.

III.

Mother, I cannot sing
fallen leaves back
onto their branches.

The Blue Dress in Mother's Closet

Her blue dress is a silk train is a river,
is water seeps into the cobblestone streets of my sleep,
is still raining,
is monsoon brocade, is winter stars stitched into puddles,
is goodbye in a flooded antique room,
is goodbye in a room of crystal bowls and crystal cups,
is the ring-ting-ring of water dripping
from the mouths of crystal bowls and crystal cups,
is the Mississippi River is a hallway,
is leaks like tears from window sills of a drowned house,
is windows open to waterfalls,
is a bed is a small boat is a ship,
is a current come to carry me in its arms through the streets,
is me floating in her dress through the streets,
is only the moon sees me floating through the streets,
is me in a blue dress out to sea,
is my mother is a moon out to sea.

Boy at Threshold

The front door kicked open
to a sky of wind-blown herons, pewter
blue wings bent back

by dark gust. If I was your blood,
I would fear this feathered dusk,
but I've always wanted to be dangerous.

The air grabs my lapel, rough-tongued
gale, and drags me free.

Daedalus, After Icarus

Boys begin to gather around the man like seagulls.
He ignores them entirely, but they follow him
from one end of the beach to the other.
Their footprints burn holes in the sand.
It's quite a sight, a strange parade:
A man with a pair of wings strapped to his arms
followed by a flock of rowdy boys.
Some squawk and flap their boney limbs.
Others try to leap now and then, stumbling
as the sand tugs at their feet. One boy pretends to fly
in a circle around the man, cawing in his face.

We don't know his name, or why he walks
along our beach, talking to the wind.
To say nothing of those wings. A woman yells
to her son, *Ask him if he'll make me a pair.*
Maybe I'll finally leave your father.
He answers our cackles with a sudden stop,
turns, and runs toward the water.
The children jump into the waves after him.
Over the sounds of their thrashes and giggles,
we hear a boy say *We don't want wings.*
We want to be fish now.

After the First Shot

I run the dark winter
coatless and a shirt of briar.

Season of black sycamore
thickets, then the startle

of open fields. Bare feet
cracking earth. Each mile

birthing three more.
There are sorrel horses

herding inside me.
In a four-legged night,

clouds sink into the trees,
refuse me morning

and mourning, but I pass
what I thought was the end

of myself. To answer
your rifle's last question:

if you ever find me,
I won't be there.

Jasper, 1998: I

in memory of James Byrd, Jr.

Go back: my throat still
   crowded with dirt
              and loose teeth
but I speak
      (tongue slick with iron)
but I speak
in the language of sharp turns.

Jasper, 1998: II

in memory of James Byrd, Jr.

Go back: I accept this ride.

Tired, don't want to walk
        home.
        It's not far, but far
enough. I accept
this ride.
        Three nice men,
white men,
        a bit too nice,
but I accept: no backseat driver.

        Smile, ride, quiet.

Could have taken
                that last turn,
but I accept these men,
        their sense of direction,
but I live
        on the other side of town.

Smile, ride, quiet.

Another turn
        I wouldn't take. This road,
back road,
wrong way,
too far.

        Smile
                with questions
                in my eyes.

Ride

      backseat, sure is
      better than walking.

Quiet

      middle of no where,
      tight lipped white men,

      no other cars around,
      no sound, but my heart.

Where (say it)

Where (louder)

WHERE

are we going?

Jasper, 1998: III

in memory of James Byrd, Jr.

Chain gang, work song, back road,
my body.
Chain gang, work song, back road,
my body.
These men play me dirty
                          tell my back to sing
or break.
Hard won rattle
          of chains
          dragged behind this truck,
louder than what little sound
          is left in my throat.

Pavement becomes skin tight
drum,
          they take my teeth
          for piano keys.

My god,
this song: one man
                    chain gang, playing this road.

          Every stick,
          every pebble: this road
                          this song.

Hear me, Jasper.
Hear me for miles.

Chain gang, work song, back road,
my body

       broken   breaking   going   gone.

Hear me
for miles

Jasper
          I'm gone.

Coyote Cry

Listen to my darkness,
        my half-eclipsed notes. Mistake them
for the sound of a lonely woman
waling as she roams the hills.   She needs you
        like I need you.
Ignore the warnings; hurry to me. Why
aren't you here yet? Can't you hear
        her trouble?
                Cold air dries her muddy footprints
        to a path of hard open mouths.
If she re-traces her steps,
the footprints will eat her. Oh, farmer.
        Ragged pines snatch her cries
and keep them.
        That's why I cry. Hurry,
little one. Climb the broken stone stairs
into the hills. Climb them
        into the night's throat.

Body & Kentucky Bourbon

In my mind's night, I go back
to your work-calloused hands, your body

and the memory of fields I no longer see.
Cheek wad of chew tobacco,

Skoal tin ring in the back pocket
of threadbare jeans, knees

worn through entirely. How to name you:
farm hand, Kentucky boy, lover.

The one who taught me to bear
the back throat burn of bourbon.

Straight, no chaser, a joke in our bed,
but I stopped laughing: all those empty bottles,

kitchen counters covered with beer cans
and broken glasses. To realize you drank

so you could face me the morning after,
the only way to choke down rage at the body

sleeping beside you. What did I know
of your father's backhand or the pine casket

he threatened to put you in? Only now,
miles and years away, do I wince at the jokes:

white trash, farmer's tan, good ole boy.
And now, alone, I see your face

at the bottom of my shot glass
before my own comes through.

In Nashville

At the Silver Saloon, you show me
what a white boy in Wrangler Jeans
can do with my moves. The electric
slide grinds with boot scootin' boogie.
Two steps to the left, a sunburned woman
outdoes me entirely, throws in some hip
just to call me out. And I feel a bit
betrayed, dancing in this crowd
of snake-skin boots and red, white, and blue
rebel tattoos with the moves I thought
I had some kind of claim to, a way
of mapping out hell with my feet.

Meridian

Cinders drift in
       from a fire we can't see.
A breeze
       of sparks, the smell of mesquite
           smoked, crackling.
It could be a family grilling
or another acre
       gone to hell. In this heat,
third week, one hundred degrees
in the shade.
       We're dry tinder.
Water won't answer our questions
anymore; turns to mirage
       when touched.
Forget the need for clothes. Heat knows
       what I want to know: the river
           of sweat through the canyon
           your back becomes
       when my tongue comes
       to cool you. Two men
on fours in this razed field, red clay
to roll in.
       You are my sky burned
to blazing, the dazzle
       before my body's exhausted
collapse,
       fingers singed,
       breath,
           blue flame.

The Fabulist

He puts my hand against his chest
so his nipple can read the lines on my palm.
He insists in his certain voice
that the beat in his chest isn't a beat at all,
but an echo: the sound of two fearful feet
heading down into some poorly lit cave
made of bats and blood red gems.
He tells me again. He's told me before.
The feet walk slower the further down they go.
No, I say, taking my hand back.
It's a heart. It's always been a heart.
I say it once for him, once for myself.
He steps back and looks at me;
he needs to tell me the story again.

Blue Prelude

Last night, the ceiling above me ached
with dance. Music dripped down the walls

like rain in an old house. My eyes followed
the couple's steps from one corner

to the other, pictured the press of two chests
against soft breathing, bodies slipping

in and out of candlelight. And the hurt
was exquisite. In my empty bed, I dreamed

the record's needle pointed into my back,
spinning me into no one's song.

Sleeping Arrangement

I.

I've decided: you will stay
under our bed, the floor

not even the space between
mattress and metal frame.

Take your hand out
from under my pillow.

And take your sheets with you.
Drag them under. Make pretend ghosts.

I can't have you rattling the bed springs
so keep still, keep quiet.

Mistake yourself for shadows.
Learn the lullabies of lint.

II.

I will do right by you:
crumbs brushed off my sheets,

white chocolate chips
or the corners of crackers.

Count on the occasional dropped grape,
a peach pit with dried yellow hairs.

I've heard some men can survive
on dust mites alone for weeks at a time.

There's a magnifying glass on the night stand,
in case it comes to that.

Prelude to Bruise

In Birmingham, said the burly man –

Boy, be
a bootblack.

Your back, blue-black.
Your body,   burning.

       I like my black boys broke, or broken.
       I like to break my black boys in.

See this burnished
brown leather belt?
You see it, boy?

       Are you broke, or broken?
       I'm gonna break your back in.

Good boy. Begin: bend
over my boot,

       (or I'll bend you over my lap – *rap, rap*)

again, bend. Better,

butt out, tongue out,
lean in.

       Now, spit shine.
       Spit polish.

My boot, black.
   Your back, blue-black.

Good boy.
Black boy, blue-black boy.
Bad boy – *rap rap.*

You've been broken in.
Begin again, bend.

Mississippi Drowning

I've lined my throat
    with the river bottom's best
    silt,

allowed my fingers to shrivel
    and be taken for crawfish.

    I've laced my eyelashes with algae.

      I blink emerald.
      I blink sea glass green.

I am whatever gleams
    just under the surface.

Scoop at my sparkle. I'll give you nothing
    but disturbed reflection.

Bring your ear to the water
    and I'll sing you

      down into my arms.

    Let me show you how

      to make your lungs
      a home for minnows, how

      to let them flicker

    like silver

    in and out of your mouth
like last words,

like air.

Room 31

Cigarette smoke
      is the smell of the last couple here,
the ghost of their stains
still
   on the sheets,
      and the bed aches
      with the weight
      of my waiting.

I've left
the door ajar, enough
       for night to push
       its tongue into the room.

     (Are you on your way?
        Where did you tell your wife
        you were going?)

Another hour –
     A couple argues
     in the next room;
     Now, moans. I want
     to see their faces.

     I want to be their bed.

Another hour –
  (You said 9.
     It's almost 12.)

I try to keep my eyes
      off the carpet. It looks
like back hair, but

if you walked in
and asked me,

I would etch your name
into the shag

with the scrape of my knees.

Cruel Body

You answer his fist   and the blow
shatters you to sparks.

Unconscious   is a better place, but swim back
to your self.

Behind a door you can't open,   he drinks
to keep loving you,

then wades out into the blue hour.

Still on the floor, waiting   for your name
to claim your mouth.

          Get up. Find your legs,
leave.

He Thinks He Can Leave Me

by leaving me,

        but even now

I walk

burning

          through the abandoned streets
          of his mind.

Lonely
little town, no sound

        but my footsteps.

I grin,
mouthful of hell

          my teeth
          soot black.

In curlicues of smoke, I sing

his name
        to the night

and his darkness

mistakes me

        for sunrise.

Eclipse of My Third Life

Hunger is who we are
under a black lacquered moon.

Undone in his flash lit arms, is this my body anymore?

Red Chinese kite in the night of my throat,
no one can see.

Unpaved road that veers
into fragments of bone, a drive only he knows.

Spine stitched to shadow's edge, I lose my head
to grass when his want walks

the length of me, king of my beheaded kingdom.

Stars are just jewelry stolen from graves, he sighs,
pressing me into loam, amaryllis shoots

already owning my dark. I'll wake, a garden
gated in April light,

my veins in every leaf.

The Poet

SAEED JONES, a 2010 Pushcart Prize Nominee, received his MFA in Creative Writing at Rutgers University – Newark. His poetry has appeared or is forthcoming in publications like *Bloom*, *Hayden's Ferry Review*, *StorySouth*, *Jubilat*, *West Branch*, *Weave*, *The Collagist*, and *Linebreak*. His blog, "For Southern Boys Who Consider Poetry," is dedicated to emerging queer poets of color.

www.saeedjones.com

The Publisher

The mission of **SIBLING RIVALRY PRESS** is to develop, publish, and promote outlaw artistic talent—those projects which inspire people to read, challenge, and ponder the complexities of life in dark rooms, under blankets by cell-phone illumination, in the backseats of cars, and on spring-day park benches next to people reading Lucie Brock-Broido and James Baldwin. We welcome manuscripts which push boundaries, sing sweetly, or inspire us to perform karaoke in drag. Not much makes us flinch.

www.siblingrivalrypress.com

CPSIA information can be obtained
at www.ICGtesting.com
Printed in the USA
LVHW112030110319
610286LV00001B/13/P